It's Your Birthday...

Let's Celebrate!

by Tim Wesemann

www.ctainc.com
It's Your Birthday...Let's Celebrate!
ISBN# 0-9718985-9-6

PRINTED IN THAILAND

To: *Christian*

It's *your* birthday,
but God has given me a gift . . .
the very special gift
of having you
in my life!

Thank you for sharing with me
your life, your faith,
and everything
that makes you,
you!

From: *Mrs. McGreeny*

Let's

This is the day the LORD has made; let us rejoice and be glad in it.

~ Psalm 118:24

Celebrate!

Happy, happy birthday! It's a day to Celebrate!

THINGS TO DO:
CELEBRATE!

WHAT SHOULD WE CELEBRATE?

First, let's celebrate that this is a special day God has made.

God created this day . . .
all over the world!
This day is special simply because
God made it!
He gives us many reasons to celebrate
on your birthday

(and on all the other days, too)!

Look around you
and see all that
God created!

Now look in the mirror. There you will see a special part of God's creation . . .

YOU!

God created you to be his special child ... someone he loves with all his heart!

You are not quite like anyone else anywhere in the world.

He created you to be different.

God brought you
into this world on
this special day!

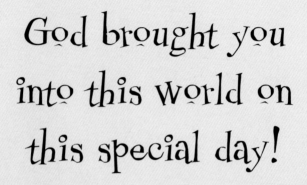

A special day . . .

A special child . . .

A special gift for
    your family,
    your friends,

and your world!

This is the special day God
chose to bring you to the world,

but he knew you long before
you were born!

He knew you and loved you
even before he created
the world!

Your life and God's love are God's birthday gifts to you!

Your God, your Creator,
says this about you:
*"… I have summoned you by name;
you are mine."*

~ Isaiah 43:1

God knew your name
before your parents knew it.
God knew the color of your skin,
eyes, and hair before anyone else
could even see you!

God knew what would make you laugh and what would cause you to cry — before he even created tears or laughter.

What amazing things you have to celebrate today — on your birthday!

You have an amazing God who created you for this special day and who created this very day for a very special you!

Sadly, God also knew you would do
things that are wrong –
things called sin.

All of us disobey God.
We sin many times each day,
even when we try not to sin.

But, because God loves you
so much, he sent someone
to rescue you from the
punishment your sins deserve.

God sent you a gift of new life, all wrapped up in a Savior named Jesus, who is God's own Son.

Jesus is the best reason to celebrate.

Jesus wants you to know, no matter what day it is, that he completely erases each and every one of your sins.

He wants you to
know he loves you.

"You Are
Loved"

Jesus saved you from

all your yesterday sins,

all your today sins, and

all your tomorrow sins.

He saved you by letting himself be killed
as punishment for your sin and then
becoming alive again to prove he has the
power to save himself (and you!) from that
punishment.

With his power he gives you a promise that you can live forever in a per-fect place called heaven – with him – as though you had never sinned!

What a great gift!

Jesus loves you so much!

Can you imagine getting a better gift than Jesus and his love?

There is nothing better than God's gift of Jesus!

While Jesus was
dying on the
cross . .

he was thinking about you!

When Jesus became alive again,
you were on his mind!

What a reason to celebrate!

What a Savior to celebrate!

What a love to celebrate!

What a day to celebrate!

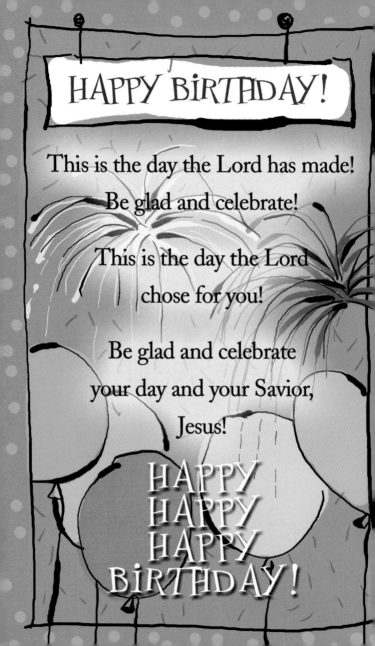

HAPPY BIRTHDAY!

This is the day the Lord has made!
Be glad and celebrate!
This is the day the Lord
chose for you!

Be glad and celebrate
your day and your Savior,
Jesus!

HAPPY
HAPPY
HAPPY
BIRTHDAY!